KU-423-631

CARDIFF
AERDYDD

LIFE SCIENCE STORIES

Animal Classification

Angela Royston

raintree
a Capstone company — publishers for children

Raintree is an imprint of Capstone Global Library Limited, a company incorporated in England and Wales having its registered office at 264 Banbury Road, Oxford OX2 7DY – Registered company number: 6695582

www.raintree.co.uk
myorders@raintree.co.uk

Produced for Raintree by Calcium
Edited by Sarah Eason and Harriet McGregor
Designed by Paul Myerscough and Geoff Ward
Picture research by Rachel Blount
Production by Victoria Fitzgerald
Originated by Capstone Global Library Limited © 2016
Printed and bound in China

ISBN 978 1 4747 1573 7
19 18 17 16 15
10 9 8 7 6 5 4 3 2 1

British Library Cataloguing in Publication Data
A full catalogue record for this book is available from the British Library.

Acknowledgements
We would like to thank the following for permission to reproduce photographs: Dreamstime: Sanja Baljkas 16, Chris Doyle 8, Editorial 29, Filmfoto 22, Fultonsphoto 24, Anthony Hathaway 27, Barbara Helgason 12, Hungchungchih 23, Laurentiu Iordach: 10, Ghm Meuffels 13, Mgkuijpers 17, Mychadre77 4, Naluphoto 15, Padede 9, Photomyeye 6, Alexey Protasov 11, Rudix 18, S100apm 5, Tomas Sereda 20, Vonmari Stoker 28, Johannes Gerhardus Swanepoel 26, Tazdevilgreg 14, Apichart Wannawal 19, Martin Zák 21, Zent 25; Shutterstock: DJ Mattaar 7.

Cover photographs reproduced with permission of: Shutterstock: Alexskopje (tl), Rob McKay (tr), Jurra8 (bl), Taboga (br).

Some words are shown in bold, **like this**. You can find out what they mean by looking in the glossary.

Contents

Life on Earth

There are millions of different types of living things, or organisms, on Earth. They include lions, fish, snakes, flowers and even **bacteria**. All living things look and behave differently. So, how do scientists make sense of it all? The answer is classification!

Grouping living things

Scientists group living things according to the way they look and live. This is called classification and it helps people to organize nature. The system includes five main groups, called kingdoms. They are animals, plants, fungi, bacteria and **protists**.

Scientists classify all living things, from the tiny animals that make up a coral reef to the different types of fish that swim around it.

The tortoise's tough shell helps it survive. **Predators** cannot crush its bony armour.

Survival story

OLD TIMER TORTOISE

A tortoise is a great survivor – it can live for 100 years or more. Tortoises are closely **related** to turtles. There have been turtles living on Earth for more than 200 million years. They were here even before the dinosaurs!

Is it an animal?

Animals can do some things that other living things cannot. They move under their own power, and they usually have senses, such as sight, hearing and touch. This helps animals to survive in the world.

What type of animal?

The animal kingdom is divided into two groups. Invertebrates are animals that have soft bodies. Animals that have bones are vertebrates and are divided into smaller groups, such as birds and **reptiles**. A species is the smallest group of all. The living things in a species are so similar they can produce young.

This great white shark is ready to catch its next meal! All animals survive by eating other animals or plants.

FLOWER OR ANIMAL?

A sea anemone looks a bit like a flower, but is an animal. It does not have roots like a plant, but clings to a rock with one large foot. It uses its stinging **tentacles** to catch food and to protect itself against **predators**. It can swim or move slowly on its single foot.

The sea anemone's mouth is found in the middle of its waving tentacles.

Changing animals

How do scientists know about animals that lived millions of years ago? The answer lies in **fossils**. When an animal dies, the shape of its bones, shell or body may be saved in the rock that forms around it. Scientists learn about ancient animals from fossils.

Changing to survive

A scientist called Charles Darwin studied fossils and living animals. He realized that a species can change over time as its surroundings change. His theory is called evolution. Sometimes species cannot change quickly enough, so become **extinct**.

This is a fossil of a dinosaur's skeleton. Fossils tell scientists a lot about how extinct animals lived.

Future story

MISSING LINKS

Scientists are always looking for "missing links". These are fossils of animals that show an important stage in their evolution. In 2009, a fossil of a seal with arms was found. It showed that sea **mammals** came from land animals, as Darwin said. Many more links are yet to be found.

Seals live mostly in the water, but they breathe in air, as land animals do. They can survive in or out of the water.

Soft bodies

The earliest animals had soft bodies and lived in the sea. Today, most species of animals are soft-bodied invertebrates. Many still live in the sea, such as jellyfish, sea anemones and squid.

Protected by a shell

Invertebrates do not have bones inside their bodies. Some do have a skeleton on the outside. A snail has a simple shell to protect its soft body. Crabs have shells with joints, like a suit of armour. The joints allow them to move their legs and claws. Insects and scorpions have jointed shells, too.

This crab uses its claws to catch and crush food. It runs sideways on six jointed legs. Its shell covers its whole body.

Survival story

GROWING NEW ARMS

Some types of starfish have **evolved** in an amazing way to survive a **predator's** attack. If they lose one or more of their five arms, they just grow new ones! The new arms grow slowly – it may take a few months or even years for them to fully grow.

A starfish has strong **suckers** underneath its arms. It uses its suckers to move around and to open shellfish to eat.

Incredible insects

Insects are invertebrates. Insects include flies, beetles and butterflies. But how can you tell if an animal is an insect? The answer is to count its legs – all insects have six legs.

How many?

There are around 1 million different species of insect, more than any other group of animals! As well as six legs, an insect has three parts to its body. It has a head, a **thorax** and an **abdomen**. It has two **antennae**, which it uses to feel and to taste. Most insects have one or two pairs of wings.

You can easily see the antennae and the three parts of this butterfly's body. Its legs are hidden beneath its wings.

People sometimes think creatures such as spiders and scorpions are insects. They are actually arachnids. Arachnids are invertebrates that have eight legs.

Future story

WHAT ELSE IS OUT THERE?

Scientists have identified about 2 million species of animals on Earth. They believe that millions more are yet to be found. Most of the undiscovered species will be insects smaller than flies and **microorganisms**. Scientists do not expect to find new types of large animals, such as lions or sharks.

Animals with backbones

Vertebrates are animals that have bones inside their bodies, including a backbone. A bony skeleton supports muscles and large body parts. This is why vertebrates can grow to be so much bigger than invertebrates.

First-ever vertebrates

The first vertebrates on Earth were fish. They appeared around 500 million years ago. Next came the other vertebrates – **amphibians**, **reptiles**, **mammals** and birds. Vertebrates are more intelligent than invertebrates because their brains are more complicated.

Fish use their muscles, fins and backbones to help them swim.

Sharks swim through the water, looking for **prey**. When they catch their prey, they use their teeth to rip it apart.

AMAZING SHARKS

Sharks are a type of fish. Their skeletons are made of cartilage, not bone. Cartilage is more flexible than bone. With their torpedo-like shape and razor-sharp teeth, they are perfectly developed to kill. No other animal attacks the biggest sharks, except for humans.

From water to land

Scientists think that around 375 million years ago the first animals moved from the sea onto the land. One of these animals was called a "fishapod". It had fins like a fish and four legs for walking on land.

Living in water, living on land

Salamanders, frogs, toads and newts are **amphibians**. They spend part of their life in the water and part of it on land. They begin life in water as eggs, which hatch into tadpoles. Tadpoles have **gills** so they can breathe underwater. As they get bigger, they grow **lungs** and breathe air.

Newts are amphibians and are **related** to salamanders. Some newts never leave the water, but others do.

Survival story

LEAKY SKIN

A frog has to keep its skin wet even when it lives on the land. Its skin is so thin that water can pass through it. Unless the frog keeps dipping itself in water, the inside of its body dries out. Frogs have to live near ponds, swamps and in water trapped in the leaves of trees.

Scaly reptiles

Lizards, snakes, turtles and crocodiles are **reptiles**. They have very dry, scaly skins. They live almost everywhere on Earth, except for very cold places. Reptiles cannot make their own heat so they take in heat from their surroundings instead.

Biggest reptiles of all

The biggest reptiles to ever live were the dinosaurs. These animals lived for around 145 million years. Dinosaurs **evolved** and changed, but then suddenly died out 66 million years ago. They may have died because Earth became much colder.

This lizard takes in heat by lying in the sun. As it becomes hotter, it starts to move around. Then it cools off in the shade.

True story

SURVIVAL SUPERSTARS

Crocodiles have out-lived dinosaurs, and even humans are not usually a threat to their survival. So, what is their secret? These animals are extremely tough. Crocodiles learn quickly and can adapt to cope with almost any change that occurs around them.

Crafty crocodiles can lie perfectly still, just under the surface of the water. Only their eyes move as they look for **prey**.

Feathery birds

Birds are the only animals that have feathers. They make their own heat and use their feathers to keep them warm and dry. All birds have wings, although some birds, such as penguins, cannot fly. Birds have beaks instead of teeth, which they use to peck food.

Laying eggs

Reptiles were the first animals to lay their eggs on land, and birds do the same. Each egg is covered with a hard shell. When the chicks hatch, the adult birds look after them until they are old enough to look after themselves.

These newborn chicks wait for their parents to bring them food. The adult birds work hard to get enough food for all their hungry chicks!

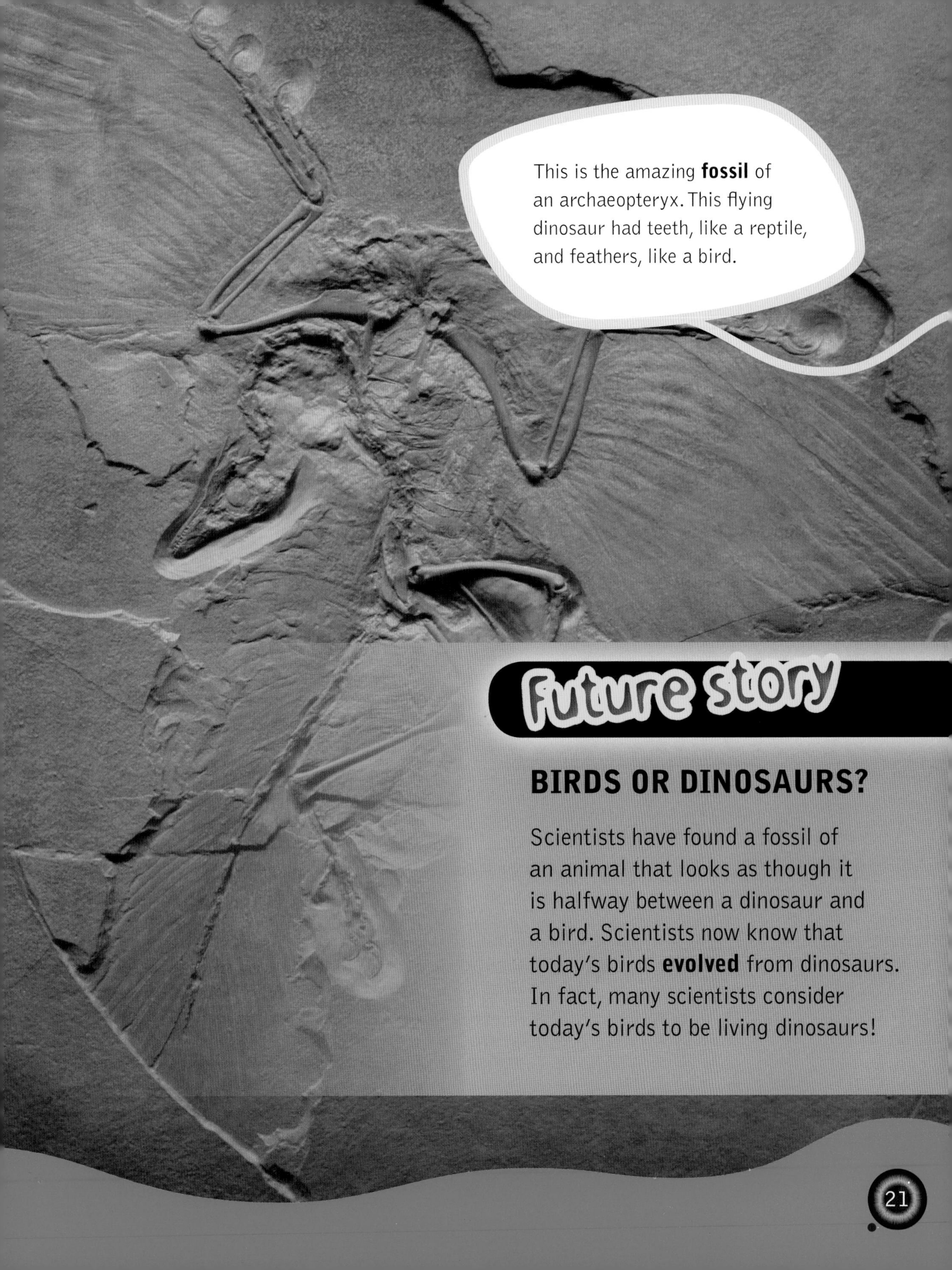

This is the amazing **fossil** of an archaeopteryx. This flying dinosaur had teeth, like a reptile, and feathers, like a bird.

Future story

BIRDS OR DINOSAURS?

Scientists have found a fossil of an animal that looks as though it is halfway between a dinosaur and a bird. Scientists now know that today's birds **evolved** from dinosaurs. In fact, many scientists consider today's birds to be living dinosaurs!

Mammal world

The only animals that feed on milk made inside their mother's body are **mammals**. The word "mammal" comes from mammary gland, the part of the female mammal's body that makes milk.

Furry families

Mammals have hair on their bodies. Some, such as bears, have thick fur. Others, such as pigs, have only a few hairs. Mammals live almost everywhere on Earth – on land, in freshwater and in the ocean. They even fly in the air – bats are mammals. Other mammals include horses, whales, mice and humans.

A young foal stays safe by keeping close to its mother. It is covered with hair and it drinks milk from its mother.

Giant pandas weigh about 90 kilograms (200 pounds). They eat bamboo and need a lot of space to live in the wild.

True story

IS A PANDA A BEAR?

There are two species of panda, the giant panda and the red panda. Scientists cannot agree on whether they are part of the family of bears or the family of raccoons. The giant panda looks like a bear and walks like a bear. The much smaller red panda is more like a raccoon.

Looking after young

Mammals look after their young as they grow up. They teach them the skills they need to survive as adults. Lions teach their cubs to chase and kill **prey**. Rabbits teach their babies to hide from **predators**.

How many babies?

Some mammals, such as whales, have one baby at a time. Others, such as cats, dogs and mice, have several babies at the same time, called a litter. Mice, rabbits and other small mammals may have more than one litter a year. Other mammals may only have one or two babies every few years.

These two lion cubs play by fighting each other. As they grow up, they will hunt for food using the skills they have learnt in play.

Survival story

BABY IN A POUCH

Marsupials are mammals that give birth to a baby that is not yet fully formed. The tiny baby crawls into the mother's pouch, where it feeds on her milk. It stays there while it grows. When it is big enough, it jumps out of the pouch to have a look around – before jumping back in!

Living in groups

Many **mammals** live in groups, which helps them to survive in different ways. Wolves and wild dogs live in packs and work together to hunt **prey**. They share the meal – but the leading male always eats first!

Safety in numbers

Plant-eating animals often stay together in large herds. A large group is less likely to be attacked than an animal on its own. Sometimes the groups are made up of just females and their young. Young male elephants usually leave the herd when they are between 10 and 12 years old.

Female elephants form a group to help each other look after the young elephants. Together they look for leaves and grass to eat.

True story

ON GUARD

Prairie dogs dig **burrows** under the grassy lands where they live. Families join together to make a group of 500 or more animals. They come above ground in the daytime to eat grass and insects. While most of the group feeds, one or two prairie dogs look out for danger.

Prairie dogs stand up tall to see all around them. When a **predator** comes close, they bark an alarm and dive into their burrow.

Top of the tree?

Monkeys, apes and humans all belong to a group called primates. They are clever animals and have more complicated brains than other **mammals**. Humans are the most intelligent of all.

Far too clever?

Humans are able to solve more difficult problems than other animals. They have invented machines and are able to write. There are a lot of humans on Earth now, while many other animals are becoming **extinct**. Humans have damaged or destroyed animals' habitats so the animals can no longer survive.

Chimpanzees are our closest relatives. Like humans, these primates are also very intelligent.

True story

WHAT NEXT?

If humans do not look after Earth, we could destroy our planet and become extinct. However, evolution is still happening. People could stop harming our planet, or another species could even take our place. Will we use our brains to change our ways so we can survive on Earth?

Glossary

abdomen part of the body that contains the stomach and gut

amphibian vertebrate that begins life in water but changes as it grows so that it can also live on land

antenna feeler that allows an insect to touch, smell, taste and hear

bacteria tiny organism that is neither a plant nor an animal

burrow hole underground in which animals live

evolve change very gradually over time

extinct no longer existing

fossil pattern in stone made by the body of a living thing

gills part of the body of a fish or tadpole that is used to breathe in water

lung part of the body that takes in air in order to breathe

mammal vertebrate that feeds its young with milk

microorganism living thing that is so small it can be seen only under a microscope

predator animal that hunts and eats other animals

prey animal that is eaten by another animal

protist microscopic organism that is not a plant or animal

related belonging to the same family or similar group of animals

reptile animal that is covered with a dry, scaly skin. A reptile is a cold-blooded animal and must take in heat from its surroundings.

sucker round part of an animal that can grip on to things

tentacle part of the body of some invertebrates, which is used to feel and grasp

thorax part of an insect's body between the head and abdomen

Find out more

Books

Adapted to Survive series, Angela Royston (Raintree, 2014)

Animal Body Parts series, Clare Lewis (Raintree, 2015)

Animal Classification series, Angela Royston (Raintree, 2015)

Websites

ngkids.co.uk/did-you-know/ten-panda-facts
Find out amazing facts about all kinds of animals – click through from pandas to black bears, or go to "Did you know?" for many other animals.

www.nhm.ac.uk/kids-only/dinosaurs
Discover the world of dinosaurs at the Natural History Museum's website.

www.oum.ox.ac.uk/thezone/animals/animalid
Visit this website for a great introduction to animal classification and try out the interactive games.

Index